AUDREY GRANT

BRIDGE AT A GLANCE

MODERN STANDARD & TWO-OVER-ONE GAME FORCE

COLOR-CODED BIDDING MESSAGES

Light Green	Forcing
Dark Green	Game Forcing
Yellow	Invitational
Red	Signoff
Orange	Conventional

THE BIDDING LADDER

The bids in order from 1♣ to 7NT.

TABS

An efficient way to find the information you need

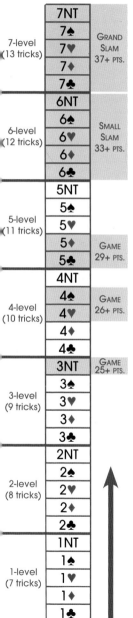

	7NT	
7-level (13 tricks)	**7♠**	GRAND SLAM 37+ PTS.
	7♥	
	7♦	
	7♣	
	6NT	
6-level (12 tricks)	**6♠**	SMALL SLAM 33+ PTS.
	6♥	
	6♦	
	6♣	
	5NT	
5-level (11 tricks)	**5♠**	
	5♥	
	5♦	GAME 29+ PTS.
	5♣	
	4NT	
4-level (10 tricks)	**4♠**	GAME 26+ PTS.
	4♥	
	4♦	
	4♣	
	3NT	GAME 25+ PTS.
3-level (9 tricks)	**3♠**	
	3♥	
	3♦	
	3♣	
	2NT	
2-level (8 tricks)	**2♠**	
	2♥	
	2♦	
	2♣	
	1NT	
1-level (7 tricks)	**1♠**	
	1♥	
	1♦	
	1♣	

THE BIDDING LADDER

OPENING THE BIDDING

HAND VALUATION

HIGH-CARD POINTS (HCP)		DISTRIBUTION POINTS	
Ace	4 points	Five-card suit	1 point
King	3 points	Six-card suit	2 points
Queen	2 points	Seven-card suit	3 points
Jack	1 point	Eight-card suit	4 points

Add the *high-card points** to the *distribution points*. If the total is 12-21, open at the one level[1,2,3].

HAND SHAPE

A *balanced* hand has no *voids*, no *singletons*, and at most one *doubleton*. There are only three balanced hand patterns:

X X X X	X X X X	X X X X X
X X X	X X X X	X X X
X X X	X X X	X X X
X X X	X X	X X
4-3-3-3	4-4-3-2	5-3-3-2

PRIORITIES AT THE ONE LEVEL

- Open 1NT with a balanced hand and 15-17 points.
  - Most experienced players add 1 *length point* for a five-card suit, so the range is actually 14^+-17
  - 1NT can be opened with a five-card major suit
- Open 1♥ or 1♠ with a five-card or longer major suit.
  - Open the *higher-ranking* of two five-card or longer suits.
- Open 1♣ or 1♦ with nothing else to do.
  - Open 1♦ with four cards in both minor suits.
  - Open 1♣ with three cards in both minor suits.

STRONG OPENING BIDS

A 2NT opening shows 20-21 points. Hands with 22 or more points or nine or more tricks are opened 2♣.

PREEMPTIVE OPENING BIDS

Weak two-bids (2♦/♥/♠) and opening bids at the three level or higher are descriptive and obstructive.

FOOTNOTES

1. In *first* or *second position*, an alternative for hand valuation is the *Guideline of 20* (see page 35).
2. In *third position* you can open lighter.
3. In *fourth position*, you can use the *Guideline of 15* (see page 35).
4. A *good suit* implies two of the top three honors or three of the top five (A-Q-x-x-x-x, Q-J-10-x-x-x).
5. Some partnerships use *Gambling 3NT* ... a solid seven-card or eight-card minor suit.

COLOR-CODED BIDDING MESSAGES

- **Light Green** *Forcing*; partner is expected to bid.
- **Dark Green** *Forcing* to at least game.
- Yellow *Invitational*; partner can bid or pass.
- **Red** *Signoff*; partner is expected to pass.
- Orange *Conventional*.

POINTS ARE ONLY A GUIDE IN THESE SUMMARIES

Hands can be valued in many different ways:

- High Cards: *High-card points* (HCPs).
- Distribution: *Length points*.
  Dummy points (shortness points).
- Playing Tricks: A *good*[4] 6-card suit is worth about five *playing tricks*.
- Other factors: 10s, 9s, (Q–J–10–9 is better than Q–J–3–2), togetherness of honors, high cards in partner's suit.

	OPENING BID	POINTS	DESCRIPTION
			Opening bids at a higher level are rare
GAME	5♦	Less than one-level opening bid	Good nine-card suit with about eight playing tricks[4]
	5♣		
	4NT	25+	Blackwood (pg 28) (rare)
GAME	4♠	Less than one-level opening bid	Good eight-card suit with about seven playing tricks[4]
	4♥		
	4♦		
	4♣		
GAME	3NT		Partnership agreement[5]
	3♠	Less than one-level opening bid	Good seven-card suit with about six playing tricks[4]
	3♥		
	3♦		
	3♣		
	2NT	20 - 21	Balanced
	2♠	5 - 10	Good six-card suit with about five playing tricks[4]
	2♥		
	2♦		
	2♣	22+	Strong, artificial; any shape (pg 26)
	1NT	15 - 17	Balanced
	1♠	12 - 21	Five-card or longer suit
	1♥		
	1♦	12 - 21	Three-card or longer suit
	1♣		

OPENING BIDS

Responding to 1♣ or 1♦

The Objective

The priority is to find an eight-card or longer major-suit *fit*. Major-suit contracts are worth more than minor-suit contracts; 4♥ or 4♠ need one less trick than 5♣ or 5♦.

With no major-suit fit, the next objective is to play in a notrump contract. Notrump contracts are worth more than minor-suit contracts and 3NT requires two fewer tricks than 5♣ or 5♦.

Responder's Priority with 6+ Points[1]

1) Bid a new suit at the one level, *forcing*[2].
   - Bid the longest suit.
   - With a choice of five-card or six-card suits, bid the *higher-ranking* suit.
   - With a choice of four-card suits, bid the *lowest-ranking* suit, responding *up the line*.
   - When responding to 1♣ with about 6-10 points, some players prefer to bypass a four-card or longer diamond suit to bid a four-card major suit.

2) Bid notrump[8].
   - 3NT = 13-15 points[4]
   - 2NT = 11-12 points[4]
   - 1NT = 6-10 points.

3) Raise opener's minor suit.
   - 13+: Start with a new suit, planning to raise later.
   - 11-12: Raise to the three level, a *limit raise*[6].
   - 6-10: Raise to the two level[6].

Footnotes

1. An opening 1♣ or 1♦ bid is not forcing, even though it could be a three-card suit.
2. A 2♣ response to 1♦ shows a five-card or longer suit and is *Two-Over-One Game Force (2/1)*. Playing *Standard*, a 2♣ response shows 11+ points and is forcing, but not to game.
3. The modern style is to use a *jump* response in a new suit (e.g. 1♦–2♠) to show a weak hand and six-card suit (weak jump shift). The classic style is to play this as a strong jump shift, showing about 17+ points, a good five-card or longer suit, and *slam* interest.
4. The classic style is 2NT, 13-15 points and 3NT, 16-18
5. Some partnerships like to use a double jump in a new suit as artificial (*splinter bid*). Example: 1♦–3♥ shows four-card or longer diamond support, 13 or more points, and a singleton or void in hearts.
6. Some partnerships play a single minor-suit raise as strong and a jump raise as weak (*inverted minors*)
7. A *Pass* usually does not carry a specific bidding message since either partner may bid later depending how the auction continues.
8. With 16+ points, start by bidding a new suit planning to show the extra strength later.

4

	RESPONSE	POINTS	DESCRIPTION
GAME	5♦	Fewer than 10	Six or more diamonds; preemptive
	4NT	20+	Blackwood: asking for aces
GAME	4♥/♠	Fewer than 10	Good seven-card or longer suit; preemptive
	4♦		Good six or more diamonds; preemptive
	4♣		Partnership agreement[5]
GAME 25+ PTS.	3NT	13 - 15	Balanced; no four-card major[4]
	3♥/♠		Partnership agreement[5]
	3♦	11 - 12	Five or more diamonds; no four-card major[6]
	3♣	4 - 7	Six or more clubs[3]
	2NT	11 - 12	Balanced; no four-card major[4]
	2♠	4 - 7	Six-card or longer suit[3]
	2♥		
	2♦	6 - 10	Five or more diamonds (usually); no major[6]
	2♣	13+	Five or more clubs (usually)[2]
	1NT	6 - 10	No four-card major
	1♠	6+	Four-card or longer suit
	1♥		
	Pass	0 - 5	Game is unlikely[1,7]

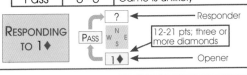

RESPONDING TO 1♦

? ← Responder
PASS | N W E S | 12-21 pts; three or more diamonds
1♦ ← Opener

	RESPONSE	POINTS	DESCRIPTION
GAME	5♣	Fewer than 10	Six or more clubs; preemptive
	4NT	20+	Blackwood: asking for aces
GAME	4♥/♠	Fewer than 10	Good seven-card or longer suit; preemptive
	4♦		Rare
	4♣		Six or more clubs; preemptive
GAME 25+ PTS.	3NT	13 - 15	Balanced; no four-card major[4]
	3♦/♥/♠		Partnership agreement[5]
	3♣	11 - 12	Five or more clubs; no four-card major[6]
	2NT	11 - 12	Balanced; no four-card major[4]
	2♠	4 - 7	Six-card or longer suit[3]
	2♥		
	2♦		
	2♣	6 - 10	Five or more clubs (usually); no four-card major[6]
	1NT	6 - 10	Balanced; no four-card major
	1♠	6+	Four-card or longer suit
	1♥		
	1♦		
	Pass	0 - 5	Game is unlikely[1,7]

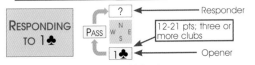

RESPONDING TO 1♣

? ← Responder
PASS | N W E S | 12-21 pts; three or more clubs
1♣ ← Opener

Responding to 1♥ or 1♠ with Support

With three-card or longer support for partner's major suit, revalue the hand using *dummy points* in place of *length points*: void – 5 points, singleton – 3 points, doubleton – 1 point. Raise to the appropriate level:

- **13+ points**   Bid a new suit and then raise to at least the game level[2,3,4].
- **11-12 points**   Four-card or longer support: *jump* to the three level, a *limit raise*.

   Three-card support: bid 1NT and then raise to the three level[7].
- **6-10 points**   Raise to the two level[1].
- **0-5 points**   Pass[1].

Responding to 1♥ or 1♠ without Support

Without support, bid a new suit if possible:

- **13+ points**   A new suit at the one or two level[5].
- **6+ points**   A new suit at the one level.

Otherwise, bid notrump:

- **13-15 points**   3NT
- **6-12 points**   1NT[7]

Footnotes

1. With five-card or longer support, *responder* can make a *preemptive* raise to game (fewer than 10 points).
2. Some partnerships use a direct response of 2NT as artificial (*Jacoby 2NT*), showing four-card or longer support and 13+ points.
3. Some partnerships use a double jump response in a new suit (e.g. 1♠–4♦) as artificial (*splinter bid*) showing four-card or longer support, 13-15 points, and a singleton or void in the suit bid.
4. A new suit at the two level without jumping is *Two Over-One Game Force* (*2/1*) after partner has opened 1♥, or 1♠, in first or second position, and the next player passes. Playing *Standard*, a new suit shows 11+ and is forcing, but not to game.
5. A new minor suit at the two level shows a four-card or longer suit (occasionally three-card); 2♥ shows a five-card or longer suit.
6. The modern style is to use a *jump* response in a new suit (e.g. 1♥–2♠) to show a weak hand (weak jump shift). The classic style is to play this as a strong jump shift, showing about 17+ points, a good five-card or longer suit, and *slam* interest.
7. Playing *2/1*, a 1NT response to a major suit shows 6-12 points and is forcing (or semi-forcing) when responder hasn't passed initially and the opponents haven't interfered. Playing *Standard*, a 1NT response is 6-10 points, non-forcing.

Color Key: ■ Forcing/Game ■ Invitational ■ Signoff ■ Conventional

	RESPONSE	POINTS	DESCRIPTION	
	4NT	20+	Blackwood: asking for aces	
GAME	4♠	Fewer than 10	Five or more spades; preemptive[1]	
	4♣/♦/♥		Partnership agreement[3]	
GAME 25+ PTS.	3NT	13 - 15	Balanced; two spades	
	3♠	11 - 12	Four or more spades	
	3♥	4 - 7	Six-card or longer suit[6]	
	3♦			
	3♣			
	2NT		Partnership agreement[2]	
	2♠	6 - 10	Three or more spades	
	2♥	13+	Five or more hearts[4]	
	2♦	13+	Four-card or longer suit[4]	Responder may have three-card spade support
	2♣			
	1NT	6 - 12	Any distribution[7]	
	Pass	0 - 5	Game is unlikely	

RESPONDING TO 1♠

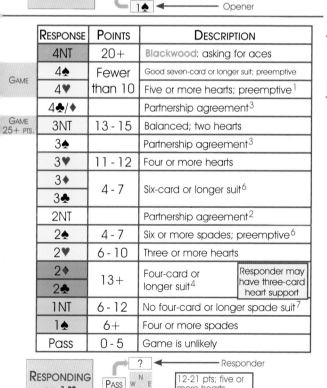

? ← Responder
PASS | N W E S | 12-21 pts; five or more spades
1♠ ← Opener

	RESPONSE	POINTS	DESCRIPTION	
	4NT	20+	Blackwood: asking for aces	
GAME	4♠	Fewer than 10	Good seven-card or longer suit; preemptive	
	4♥		Five or more hearts; preemptive[1]	
	4♣/♦		Partnership agreement[3]	
GAME 25+ PTS.	3NT	13 - 15	Balanced; two hearts	
	3♠		Partnership agreement[3]	
	3♥	11 - 12	Four or more hearts	
	3♦	4 - 7	Six-card or longer suit[6]	
	3♣			
	2NT		Partnership agreement[2]	
	2♠	4 - 7	Six or more spades; preemptive[6]	
	2♥	6 - 10	Three or more hearts	
	2♦	13+	Four-card or longer suit[4]	Responder may have three-card heart support
	2♣			
	1NT	6 - 12	No four-card or longer spade suit[7]	
	1♠	6+	Four or more spades	
	Pass	0 - 5	Game is unlikely	

RESPONDING TO 1♥

? ← Responder
PASS | N W E S | 12-21 pts; five or more hearts
1♥ ← Opener

Responder has two decisions to make:

- How High: *Partscore*, *game*, or *slam*.
- Where: ♣, ♦, ♥, ♠, or notrump.

Opener has shown a narrow range of strength and has promised a *balanced* or *semi-balanced* hand... at least two cards in every suit. For example:

RESPONDING TO 1NT WHEN RESPONDER DECIDES TO PLAY IN NOTRUMP		
RESPONDER'S POINT COUNT	HOW HIGH?	BID
22+	Grand slam	7NT
20-21	Invite grand slam	5NT
18-19	Small slam	6NT
16-17	Invite small slam	4NT
10-15	Game	3NT
8-9	Invite game	2NT
0-7	Partscore	Pass

Stayman is used to search for an eight-card major suit fit. *Transfer bids* can also be used. (See pages 24-25.)

OPENER'S REBID

- If responder makes a *signoff* bid, opener passes.
- If responder makes an *invitational* bid, opener passes with a minimum and accepts with a maximum. For example, if responder raises 1NT to 2NT, opener passes with 15-16 and bids 3NT with 17 ... or a good 16.
- If responder makes a *forcing* bid, opener makes a descriptive rebid.

FOOTNOTES

1. Stayman and transfers can be used after a 2NT opening, or 2♣-2♦-2NT/3NT.
2. Stayman can be used with 0-7 points when short in clubs, planning to pass opener's rebid.
3. With four hearts and four spades, opener bids 2♥ in response to Stayman, bidding up the line.
4. Other meanings can be assigned to jump responses of 3♣ and 3♦ (signoff, or forcing).
5. Some partnerships also use transfer bids at the four level (*Texas transfers*).
6. Not playing transfers, 2♦, 2♥, 2♠ is natural, five or more cards, signoff; 3♥, 3♠, forcing to game.

Color Key: ■ Forcing/Game ▨ Invitational ■ Signoff ■ Conventional

	RESPONSE	POINTS	DESCRIPTION
SLAM 33+ PTS.	6NT	13 - 15	Balanced (usually)
	5NT	16	Inviting grand slam
	4NT	11 - 12	Inviting opener to bid slam
GAME 26+ PTS.	4♠	4 - 10	Six-card or longer suit
	4♥	4 - 10	Six-card or longer suit[5]
	4♦		Partnership agreement[5]
	4♣	13+	Gerber: asking for aces
GAME 25+ PTS.	3NT	4 - 10	Balanced (usually)
	3♠		Partnership agreement[6]
	3♥	0+	Transfer to 3♠; five or more spades[1,6]
	3♦	0+	Transfer to 3♥; five or more hearts[1]
	3♣	4+	Stayman: asking for a major suit[1]
	Pass	0 - 3	Balanced (usually)

RESPONDING TO 2NT

? ← Responder
PASS
20-21 pts; balanced
2NT ← Opener

	RESPONSE	POINTS	DESCRIPTION
SLAM 33+ PTS.	6NT	18 - 19	Balanced (usually)
	5NT	20 - 21	Inviting grand slam
	4NT	16 - 17	Inviting opener to bid slam
GAME 26+ PTS.	4♠	10 - 15	Six-card or longer suit
	4♥	10 - 15	Six-card or longer suit[5]
	4♦		Partnership agreement[5]
	4♣	18+	Gerber: asking for aces
GAME 25+ PTS.	3NT	10 - 15	Balanced (usually)
	3♠	16+	Six-card or longer suit; slam interest
	3♥	16+	
	3♦	8 - 9	Good six-card suit[4]
	3♣	8 - 9	
	2NT		Balanced (usually)
	2♠	0+	Relay to 3♣; six or more clubs or diamonds[6]
	2♥	0+	Transfer to 2♠; five or more spades[6]
	2♦	0+	Transfer to 2♥; five or more hearts[6]
	2♣	8+	Stayman: asking for a major suit
	Pass	0 - 7	Balanced (usually)[2]

RESPONDING TO 1NT

? ← Responder
PASS
15-17 pts; balanced
1NT ← Opener

OPENER'S REBID AFTER OPENING 1♣ OR 1♦

Opener considers whether *responder's* bidding message is forcing[7], invitational, or signoff. Opener generally wants to further describe the strength and *distribution* of the hand. Opener puts the hand into one of three approximate categories, revaluing with *dummy points* with support for responder's suit.

12	13	14	15	16	17	18	19	20	21

MINIMUM	MEDIUM	MAXIMUM

REBID WITH MINIMUM VALUES (12-16)

- Raise responder's suit to the cheapest level with four-card, or occasionally three-card, support.
- Bid a new suit. At the two level it must be *lower-ranking*[2].
- Rebid a six-card or longer suit at the cheapest level.
- Bid notrump or pass responder's notrump bid with a *balanced* hand and 12-14 points[1].
- Pass responder's minimum raise[1].

REBID WITH MEDIUM VALUES (17-18)

- *Jump* raise responder's suit with four-card or longer support.
- Bid a new suit[2,6].
- Jump rebid with a good six-card or longer suit.
- Raise responder's notrump bid.

REBID WITH MAXIMUM VALUES (19-21)

- Jump to game in responder's suit with four-card or longer support.
- Jump in a new suit – jump shift – or *reverse* in a new *higher-ranking* suit[6].
- Jump to game in a good seven-card or longer suit.
- Jump to 2NT with a balanced hand of 18-19 points.

FOOTNOTES

1. Opener can pass if responder raised opener's suit or made an invitational bid in notrump.
2. A new lower-ranking suit rebid at the cheapest level has a wide range of 12-18 points.
3. When responder raises opener's suit to the two level, opener can make a *game try* by bidding a new suit – forcing – or 2NT.
4. The modern style is a *re-raise* of opener's suit to the three level is competitive rather than a game try.
5. Some partnerships use a double jump rebid in a new suit as artificial, a splinter bid (e.g. 1♦-1♥–4♣).
6. A reverse – opener's bid of a new suit at the two level higher-ranking than opener's first suit – is forcing and shows 17+ points.
7. A response of 2♣ to a 1♦ opening is game-forcing. Since the partnership is committed to game, opener focuses on describing the distribution: supporting responder's clubs, bidding a second suit, rebidding a six-card or longer suit, or bidding notrump. Any extra strength can be shown later.

	REBID	POINTS	DESCRIPTION
GAME 25+ PTS.	3NT	20 - 21	Semi-balanced (didn't open 2NT)
	3♦	17 - 18	Six or more diamonds
	3♣	19 - 21	Five or more diamonds; four or more clubs
	2NT	18 - 19	Balanced or semi-balanced
	2♠	17 - 21	Five or more diamonds; four spades[6]
	2♥		Five or more diamonds; four hearts[6]
	2♦	12 - 16	Six or more diamonds
	2♣	12 - 18	Five or more diamonds; four or more clubs
	Pass	12 - 14	Balanced or semi-balanced[1]

OPENER'S REBID AFTER A 1NT RESPONSE

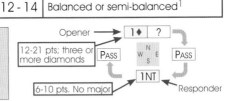

Opener → 1♦ ?
12-21 pts; three or more diamonds — PASS
1NT ← Responder
6-10 pts. No major

	REBID	POINTS	DESCRIPTION
GAME 25+ PTS.	4♥	19 - 21	Four hearts
	4♦		Partnership agreement[5]
	4♣		
GAME 25+ PTS.	3NT		Partnership agreement
	3♠		Partnership agreement[5]
	3♥	17 - 18	Four hearts
	3♦		Partnership agreement[5]
	3♣	17 - 18	Six-card or longer suit
	2NT	18 - 19	Balanced; fewer than four hearts
	2♠	19 - 21	Five or more clubs; four spades
	2♥	12 - 16	Three or more hearts; usually four
	2♦	17 - 21	Five or more clubs; four diamonds[6]
	2♣	12 - 16	Six or more clubs
	1NT	12 - 14	Balanced; fewer than four spades or four hearts
	1♠	12 - 18	Four spades; fewer than four hearts

OPENER'S REBID AFTER A NEW SUIT RESPONSE

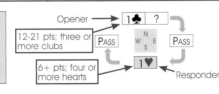

Opener → 1♣ ?
12-21 pts; three or more clubs — PASS
1♥ ← Responder
6+ pts; four or more hearts

OPENER'S REBID AFTER
OPENING 1♣ OR 1♦

When responder didn't pass originally and bids a new suit at the two level with no interference from the opponents, it is game-forcing when playing *Two-Over-One Game Force* (*2/1*). Since the partnership is committed to game, opener focuses on describing the distribution: supporting responder's suit, bidding a second suit, rebidding a six-card or longer suit, or bidding notrump. Any extra strength can be shown later.

Otherwise, responder's bidding message is simply forcing, invitational, or signoff. Opener further describes both the strength and distribution, revaluing with dummy points with support for responder's suit.

Clarifying Strength and Shape with:
Minimum Values (12-16)[1]

- Raise responder's suit to the cheapest level with four-card, occasionally three-card, support.
- Bid a new suit. If it is at the two level it must be *lower-ranking*[2].
- Rebid a six-card or longer suit at the cheapest level.
- Bid notrump with a *balanced* hand (12-14).

Medium Values (17-18)

- *Jump* raise responder's suit with four-card or longer support.
- Bid a new suit[2,4,6].
- Jump rebid with a good six-card or longer suit.

Maximum Values (19-21)

- Jump to game in responder's suit with four-card or longer support.
- Jump in a new lower-ranking suit – jump shift – or *reverse* in a new *higher-ranking* suit[6].
- Jump to game in a good seven-card or longer suit.
- Jump to 2NT with a balanced hand of 18-19 points.

Footnotes

1. Opener can pass if responder raised opener's suit.
2. A new suit rebid at the cheapest level has a wide range of 12-18 points – minimum or medium.
3. When responder raises opener's suit to the two level, opener can make a *game try* by bidding a new suit – forcing – asking for help in that suit – high cards or shortness.
4. Opener's rebid of the original suit at the three level after it is raised to the two level by responder, is competitive in the modern style rather than a game try. A new suit or 2NT is a game try.
5. Some partnerships use a double jump rebid in a new suit as artificial (*splinter bid*) (e.g. 1♥-1♠–4♦).
6. A reverse – a new suit at the two level higher-ranking than opener's first suit – is forcing and shows 17+ points.

Color Key: ■ Forcing/Game □ Invitational ▨ Signoff ▦ Conventional

	Rebid	Points	Description
Game 26+ pts.	4♥	19 – 21	Seven or more hearts
			Other rebids are rare
	3♥	17 – 18	Six or more hearts
	3♦	19 – 21	Five or more hearts; four or more diamonds
	3♣		Five or more hearts; four or more clubs
	2NT	18 – 19	Balanced or semi-balanced
	2♠	17 – 21	Five or more hearts; four spades[6]
	2♥	12 – 16	Six or more hearts
	2♦	12 – 18	Five hearts; three or more diamonds[2]
	2♣		Five hearts; three or more clubs[2]

OPENER'S REBID AFTER A 1NT RESPONSE

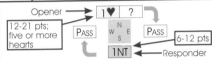

	Rebid	Points	Description
Game 26+ pts.	4♠	19 – 21	Five or more hearts; four spades
	4♥		Seven or more hearts
	4♣/♦		Partnership agreement[5]
Game 25+ pts.	3NT		Partnership agreement
	3♠	17 – 18	Five or more hearts; four spades
	3♥		Six or more hearts
	3♦	19 – 21	Five or more hearts; four or more diamonds
	3♣		Five or more hearts; four or more clubs
	2NT	18 – 19	Balanced; two or three spades
	2♠	12 – 16	Five or more hearts; ideally four spades
	2♥		Six or more hearts
	2♦	12 – 18	Five or more hearts; four or more diamonds[2]
	2♣		Five or more hearts; four or more clubs[2]
	1NT	12 – 14	Balanced; fewer than four spades

OPENER'S REBID AFTER A NEW SUIT

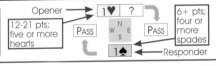

	Rebid	Points	Description
Game 26+ pts.	4♥	19 – 21	Game is likely
	3♠/4♣/♦		Partnership agreement[5]
	3♥	12 – 16	Competitive with six or more hearts[4]
	2♠/3♣/♦	17 – 18	Game try[3]
	2NT	17 – 18	Balanced; inviting game[4]
	Pass	12 – 16	Game is unlikely[1]

OPENER'S REBID AFTER A RAISE

Copyright © 2023 Audrey Grant's Better Bridge Corp.

RESPONDER'S REBID

RESPONDER'S OBJECTIVE

Responder has heard two descriptive bids from opener and can usually decide How High and Where to place the contract.

If responder's first bid was game-forcing, any rebid below the game level is still forcing, so there's no need to jump to game if there is still uncertainty about the best contract. Responder's options are:

- Agree on a trump suit if that hasn't happened already.
- Rebid a six-card or longer suit.
- Suggest notrump if there is no major-suit fit.
- Bid the fourth suit to get more information from opener.

When responder initially made a forcing or invitational bid, responder determines:

HOW HIGH

OPENER'S POINT COUNT	RESPONDER'S POINT COUNT		
	6-10 points	11-12 points	13-16 points
19-21	Get to *game*	Invite *slam*	Get to slam
17-18	6-7 Settle for *partscore* 8-10 Get to game	Get to game	Invite slam
12-16	Settle for partscore. 1NT or an *old suit* at the two level.	Invite game. 2NT or an old suit at the three level is *invitational.*[1]	Get to game[1]

WHERE

At the game level, responder's priority is an eight-card or longer major suit *fit*, 4♥ or 4♠. Otherwise, 3NT is usually preferable to 5♣ or 5♦. At the partscore or slam level, any eight-card or longer fit is okay. Otherwise, notrump.

FOOTNOTES

1. A new suit by responder is *forcing*. One exception is after opener's rebid of 1NT. Then responder's second suit, if *lower-ranking* than responder's first suit, is not forcing. Responder's jump in a new suit is forcing.

Color Key: ■ Forcing/Game □ Invitational ■ Signoff ■ Conventional

	REBID	POINTS	DESCRIPTION
SLAM 33+ PTS.	6♠	13 - 15	Slam is likely
			Other rebids are rare
	4NT	13+	Blackwood: asking for aces
GAME 26+ PTS.	Pass	6 - 12	Slam is unlikely

RESPONDER'S REBID WHEN OPENER IS MAXIMUM

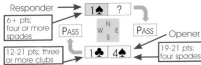

Responder → 1♠ ?
6+ pts; four or more spades | PASS | N W E S | PASS ← Opener
12-21 pts; three or more clubs | 1♣ 4♠ ← 19-21 pts; four spades

	REBID	POINTS	DESCRIPTION
	4NT	15+	Blackwood: asking for aces
GAME 26+ PTS.	4♠		Partnership agreement
	4♥	8 - 14	No slam interest
	4♦	15+	Slam interest, control-showing
	4♣		
GAME 25+ PTS.	3NT	8 - 14	Rare
	3♠	15+	Slam interest, control-showing
	Pass	6 - 7	Four or more hearts; no interest in game

RESPONDER'S REBID WHEN OPENER IS MEDIUM

Responder → 1♥ ?
6+ pts; four or more hearts | PASS | N W E S | PASS ← Opener
12-21 pts; three or more clubs | 1♣ 3♥ ← 17-18 pts; four hearts

	REBID	POINTS	DESCRIPTION
	4NT	19+	Blackwood: asking for aces
GAME 26+ PTS.	4♠	13 - 16	Seven or more spades; fewer than three hearts
	4♥		Four or more spades; two or more hearts
	4♣/♦		Partnership agreement
GAME 25+ PTS.	3NT	13 - 16	Four or five spades; fewer than three hearts
	3♠	11 - 12	Six or more spades; fewer than three hearts
	3♥		Four or more spades; two or more hearts
	3♦	13+	Four or more spades; four or more diamonds[1]
	3♣		Four or more spades; four or more clubs[1]
	2NT	11 - 12	Balanced; interest in game
	2♠	6 - 10	Six or more spades; no interest in game
	Pass		Four or five spades; no interest in game

RESPONDER'S REBID WHEN OPENER IS MINIMUM

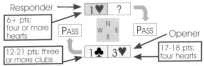

Responder → 1♠ ?
6+ pts; four or more spades | PASS | N W E S | PASS | 12-16 pts; six or more spades
12-21 pts; five or more hearts | 1♥ 2♥ ← Opener

WEAK TWOS AND OTHER PREEMPTIVE OPENINGS

Preemptive bids and responses are based on *playing tricks* rather than *high-card points*.

PREEMPTIVE OPENING BIDS

An opening bid of 2♦, 2♥, or 2♠ shows:
- A *good* six-card suit
- 5-10 points
- About five playing tricks non-vulnerable; about six playing tricks *vulnerable*.

An opening bid of 3♣, 3♦, 3♥, or 3♠ shows:
- A good seven-card suit
- Less than the values for a one-level opening bid
- About six playing tricks non-vulnerable; about seven playing tricks vulnerable.

Preemptive bids can also be made at higher levels.

RESPONDER'S PRIORITY AFTER OPENER'S PREEMPT

1) *Responder* first COUNTS TRICKS:
   - If there are likely to be enough combined tricks for game, responder bids *game*.
   - With no fit for partner's suit, responder should avoid getting too high, even with a good hand.
2) If there are not enough tricks for game, responder COUNTS TRUMPS[1] and:
   - Raises to the level corresponding to the number of combined trumps.
3) If unsure, responder can get more information by making a *forcing* bid:
   - A new suit below the game level.
   - 2NT (artificial) after a weak two-bid.

OPENER'S REBID AFTER A 2NT RESPONSE

- With a minimum weak two-bid, 5-7, rebid the suit at the three level.
- With a maximum weak two bid, 8-10, a new suit shows a feature, an Ace or King. 3NT shows a solid suit.

PREEMPTOR'S REBID

A *preemptive* opening bid gives an accurate description, leaving further decisions up to responder. Opener bids again only if responder makes a forcing bid.

FOOTNOTE

1. Based on a *Corollary to the Law of Total Tricks*: Without enough tricks for game, "Compete to the level of the number of combined trumps."

Color Key: ▨ Forcing/Game ☐ Invitational ▨ Signoff ▨ Conventional

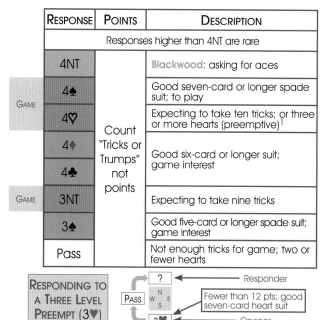

RESPONSE	POINTS	DESCRIPTION
Responses higher than 4NT are rare		
4NT	Count "Tricks or Trumps" not points	Blackwood: asking for aces
4♠		Good seven-card or longer spade suit; to play
4♡		Expecting to take ten tricks; or three or more hearts (preemptive)[1]
4♦		Good six-card or longer suit; game interest
4♣		
3NT		Expecting to take nine tricks
3♠		Good five-card or longer spade suit; game interest
Pass		Not enough tricks for game; two or fewer hearts

RESPONDING TO A THREE LEVEL PREEMPT (3♥)

? ← Responder
PASS — Fewer than 12 pts; good seven-card heart suit
3♥ ← Opener

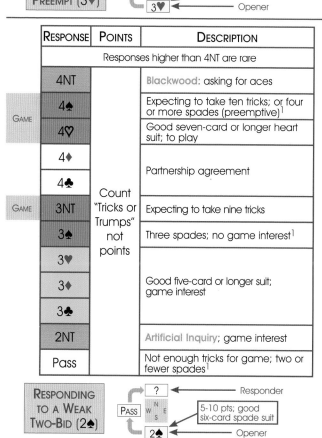

RESPONSE	POINTS	DESCRIPTION
Responses higher than 4NT are rare		
4NT	Count "Tricks or Trumps" not points	Blackwood: asking for aces
4♠		Expecting to take ten tricks; or four or more spades (preemptive)[1]
4♡		Good seven-card or longer heart suit; to play
4♦		Partnership agreement
4♣		
3NT		Expecting to take nine tricks
3♠		Three spades; no game interest[1]
3♥		Good five-card or longer suit; game interest
3♦		
3♣		
2NT		Artificial Inquiry; game interest
Pass		Not enough tricks for game; two or fewer spades[1]

RESPONDING TO A WEAK TWO-BID (2♠)

? ← Responder
PASS — 5-10 pts; good six-card spade suit
2♠ ← Opener

OVERCALLS AND ADVANCES

OBJECTIVES OF OVERCALLING

- Compete for the contract.
- Interfere with the opponents' auction.
- Help the partnership find the best defense.

REQUIREMENTS FOR A SIMPLE OVERCALL[6]

Distribution: *Good* five-card or any six-card or longer suit.

Strength[1]: 13-17 points at the two level or higher
7-17 points at the one level.

ADVANCING AN OVERCALL WITH SUPPORT[2]

10+ points: *Cuebid* the opponents' suit.

6-9 points: Raise with three-card support.

0-9 points: *Jump* raise with four-card support.
Bid game with five-card or longer support.

ADVANCING IN A NEW SUIT[3]

Distribution: Good five-card or six-card or longer suit.

Strength: 11+ points at the two level
6+ points at the one level.

ADVANCING IN NOTRUMP

15+ points: Cuebid then bid notrump.

12-14 points: Jump in notrump.

7-11 points: Bid notrump at the cheapest level.

REQUIREMENTS FOR A 1NT OVERCALL

Distribution: *Balanced. Stoppers* in opponents' suit.

Strength: 15-18 points.

REQUIREMENTS FOR A PREEMPTIVE JUMP OVERCALL

Distribution: Good eight-card suit at the four level
Good seven-card suit at the three level
Good six-card suit at the two level.

Strength: A weak hand (*preemptive*).

FOOTNOTES

1. With a hand too strong to overcall, start with a *takeout double* and then bid the suit or notrump.
2. When valuing for a raise, *advancer* counts *dummy points: void* – 5; *singleton* – 3; *doubleton* –1.
3. A new suit advance is not forcing, although some partnerships prefer to treat it as forcing.
4. Some partnerships use a cuebid of the opponents' suit to show a two-suited hand (*Michaels Cuebid*). A jump in the opponents' suit can be treated as natural.
5. Some partnerships use a jump overcall of 2NT to show a two-suited hand (*unusual notrump*).
6. With a hand unsuitable for an overcall (or a takeout double), pass ... even with 13+ points.

Color Key: ▓ Forcing/Game ░ Invitational ▓ Signoff ▓ Conventional

	ADVANCE	POINTS	DESCRIPTION
		Other advances are rare	
GAME	4♥	Fewer than 10	Five or more hearts (preemptive)
	3♠/4♣/♦		Partnership agreement
	3♥	Fewer than 10	Four hearts (preemptive)
	3♣/♦		Partnership agreement
	2NT	12 - 14	Balanced; stopper in clubs
	2♠		Partnership agreement
	2♥	6 - 9	Three hearts
	2♦	11+	Good five-card or longer diamond suit[3]
	2♣	10+	Cuebid; three or more hearts (usually)
	1NT	7 - 11	Balanced (usually); stopper in clubs
	1♠	6+	Good five-card or longer spade suit[3]
	Pass	0+	No fit (usually)

ADVANCING AN OVERCALL

? ← Advancer

PASS W N S E ← 1♣ ← Opener

Overcaller → 1♥ ← 7-17 pts; five or more hearts

	ADVANCE	POINTS	DESCRIPTION
		Overcalls higher than 4♠ are rare	
GAME	4♠	Fewer than 10	Good eight-card suit
GAME	4♥		
	4♦		Partnership agreement
	4♣		Good eight-card club suit
GAME	3NT		Rare
	3♠	Fewer than 10	Good seven-card suit (preempt)
	3♥		
	3♦		Partnership agreement[4]
	3♣		Good seven-card club suit (preempt)
	2NT		Partnership agreement[5]
	2♠	5 - 11	Good six-card suit (preempt)
	2♥		
	2♦		Partnership agreement[4]
	2♣	13 - 17	Good five-card or longer club suit
	1NT	15 - 18	Balanced; stoppers in diamonds
	1♠	7 - 17	Five-card or longer suit (usually good suit)
	1♥		
	Pass	0+	Unsuitable for overcall or double[6]

OVERCALLS AFTER A 1♦ OPENING BID

Opener → 1♦ W N S E → ? ← Overcaller

OVERCALLS AND ADVANCES

Takeout Doubles and Advances

Requirements for a *Takeout Double*[2,3,4]

Distribution: Support for the unbid suits[1].
- At least three-card support
- Preferably four-card support.

Strength: 13+ points, counting *dummy points*: *void* – 5; *singleton* – 3; *doubleton* –1.

Advancing a Takeout Double[5]

12+ points: Get the partnership to game.

9-11 points: Make an *invitational* bid by jumping a level.

0-8 points: Bid at the cheapest level.

Advancing in Notrump

With strength in the opponents' suit and no better option, bid notrump using the following ranges:

13+ points: Bid *game* in notrump.

11-12 points: Bid notrump, jumping a level.

6-10 points: Bid notrump at the cheapest level.

Advancer's Forcing Bid

When *advancer* needs more information to decide How High and Where to play, a *cuebid* of the opponents' suit is *forcing*.

Rebids by the Takeout Doubler

The takeout doubler's strength falls approximately into these ranges:

13	14	15	16	17	18	19+
Minimum				Medium		Maximum

The takeout doubler combines this information with the approximate strength shown by advancer to decide whether to bid again.

Footnotes

1. A takeout double can also be made with a hand too strong for a simple *overcall*, about 18+.
2. Double of a notrump opening bid is for *penalty*.
3. A takeout double can be made after both opponents have bid or if the doubler is a *passed hand*. It still shows support for the unbid suits.
4. The partnership has to agree how high to play takeout doubles, typically through 4♥ or 4♠. A higher-level double is then for penalty.
5. Advancer must bid if right-hand opponent passes except with enough length and strength in the opponents' suit to want to defend for penalties (rare).

	REBID	POINTS	DESCRIPTION
		Other rebids by the takeout doubler are rare	
GAME	4♥	22+	Four or more hearts
	3♥	19 - 21	Four or more hearts; strongly inviting game
	3♣/♦		Partnership agreement
	2NT	22 - 24	Balanced
	2♠		Partnership agreement
	2♥	17 - 18	Four or more hearts; inviting game
	2♦	19+	Cuebid; asking for more information
	2♣	18+	Five or more clubs; too strong to overcall 2♣
	1NT	19 - 21	Balanced; too strong to overcall 1NT
	1♠	18+	Five or more spades; too strong to overcall 1♠
	Pass	13 - 16	Game is unlikely

DOUBLER'S REBID AFTER A MINIMUM ADVANCE

13+ pts; support for the unbid suits[1]

Double ? ← Takeout Doubler

1♦ Pass | W N S E | PASS

Opener

Advancer → 1♥

0-8 pts; four or more hearts

	ADVANCE	POINTS	DESCRIPTION
GAME 29+ PTS.	5♦	12+	Five or more diamonds
	5♣		Five or more clubs
	4NT	20+	Blackwood (rare)
GAME 26+ PTS.	4♠	12+	Four or more spades
	4♥		Rare
	4♦	4 - 8	Six-card or longer suit; preemptive (rare)
	4♣		
GAME 25+ PTS.	3NT	13+	Balanced; stoppers in hearts
	3♠	4 - 8	Six or more spades; preemptive (rare)
	3♥		Rare
	3♦	9 - 11	Four-card or longer suit; inviting game
	3♣		
	2NT	11 - 12	Balanced; stoppers in hearts
	2♠	9 - 11	Four-card or longer suit; inviting game
	2♥	10+	Cuebid (artificial); asking doubler for more information)
	2♦	0 - 8	Four-card or longer suit
	2♣		
	1NT	6 - 10	Balanced; stoppers in hearts
	1♠	0 - 8	Four or more spades
	Pass	6+	Convert to penalty double (rare)[5]

ADVANCING A TAKEOUT DOUBLE

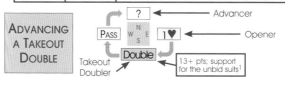

? ← Advancer

PASS | W N S E | 1♥ ← Opener

Takeout Doubler

Double

13+ pts; support for the unbid suits[1]

THE COMPETITIVE AUCTION
RESPONDER'S ACTION AFTER AN OVERCALL

When partner opens the bidding and the next player *overcalls*, *responder* can:

- Make the same response that would have been made without the overcall, if possible.
- Make a suitable alternative response if the overcall interfered with responder's original choice.
- Use the new options available after an overcall:
  - Make a *preemptive* jump raise of opener's suit with four-card or longer support and a weak hand, 0-9, including *dummy points*.
  - Cuebid the opponents' suit to show support for opener's suit and 11+ points.
  - Make a negative (takeout) double to ideally show support for the two unbid suits and enough strength to compete[1].

RESPONDER'S ACTION AFTER A TAKEOUT DOUBLE

When partner opens the bidding and the next player makes a *takeout double*, responder can:

- Redouble with 10+ high-card points[2].
- Make a preemptive jump raise of opener's suit with four-card or longer support and a weak hand, 0-9 including dummy points.
- Bid a new suit at the two level with fewer than 10 points. This is not *forcing*[3].

ADVANCER'S ACTIONS IN A COMPETITIVE AUCTION

When partner overcalls or doubles, *advancer* should strive to compete even if responder bids.

OPENER'S ACTIONS IN A COMPETITIVE AUCTION

Opener chooses a rebid based on responder's action. Opener can also use competitive calls such as the double.

THE PENALTY DOUBLE

A double is for *penalty* if it is a:

- Double of an opponent's opening 1NT or 2NT
- Double at the game level or higher (as agreed).

FOOTNOTES

1. The partnership needs to agree the level through which negative doubles apply, typically 3♠.
2. Some partnerships use a jump to 2NT to show 10+ points with four-card or longer support for partner.
3. After a takeout double, a new suit by responder at the one level is forcing, but not at the two level.
4. Opener is usually expected to pass a redouble waiting to see what type of hand responder holds.

RESPONSE	POINTS	DESCRIPTION
	Other responses are rare	
3NT	13 - 16	Balanced; some strength in spades
3♥/♠		Partnership agreement
3♦	Fewer than 10	Four or more diamonds; preemptive
3♣		Partnership agreement
2NT	11 - 12	Balanced; some strength in spades
2♠	11+	Cuebid; four or more diamonds
2♥	11+	Five or more hearts
2♦	6 - 10	Four or more diamonds
2♣	11+	Five or more clubs
1NT	6 - 10	Balanced; some strength in spades
Double	6+	Four or more hearts and ideally four or more clubs
Pass	0+	0-5 points or no convenient bid with 6+

GAME 25+ PTS (label beside 3NT row)

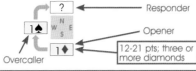

RESPONDER'S ACTIONS AFTER AN OVERCALL

Responder — ?
Opener — 1♠
Overcaller
1♦ — 12-21 pts; three or more diamonds

RESPONSE	POINTS	DESCRIPTION
	Other responses are rare	
4♥	Fewer than 10	Five or more hearts; preemptive
4♣/♦		Partnership agreement
3♠/3NT		
3♥	Fewer than 10	Four hearts; preemptive
3♣/♦		Partnership agreement
2NT		Partnership agreement[2]
2♠		Partnership agreement
2♥	6 - 10	Three or more hearts
2♦	Fewer than 10	Six-card or longer suit[3]
2♣		
1NT	6 - 10	Balanced; fewer than three hearts
1♠	6+	Four or more spades[3]
Redouble	10+	Any distribution[4]
Pass	0-5	

GAME (label beside 4♥ row)

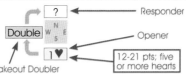

RESPONDER'S ACTIONS AFTER A DOUBLE

Responder — ?
Double
Opener
Takeout Doubler
1♥ — 12-21 pts; five or more hearts

Two popular conventions used after notrump openings are *Stayman* and *transfers*. A **conventional** call sacrifices the natural meaning of a bid in exchange for a better description of the partnership hands.

STAYMAN

Stayman is used to uncover an eight-card major suit *fit* after a 1NT opening bid[1]. With 8 or more points[2] and at least one four-card major, *responder* bids 2♣.

OPENER'S REBID		
	2♠	Four-card or longer spade suit
	2♥	Four-card or longer heart suit[3]
	2♦	No four-card or longer major

Responder then decides How HIGH and WHERE.

TRANSFERS

Transfers are used to have the weaker hand as dummy and to give responder additional options.

- 2♦ asks opener to bid 2♥.
- 2♥ asks opener to bid 2♠.
- 2♠ asks opener to bid 3♣. Responder may then pass or bid 3♦ to sign off in diamonds.

Responder then decides How HIGH and WHERE.

WHEN TO USE STAYMAN AND TRANSFERS AFTER 1NT

# CARDS IN MAJOR	RESPONDER'S POINT COUNT		
	0-7 points	8-9 points	10+ points
Six or more	Transfer and pass	Transfer and raise	Transfer and bid game
Five cards	Transfer and Pass	Transfer and bid 2NT	Transfer and bid 3NT
Four cards	Pass	2♣ Stayman	2♣ Stayman
Three or fewer	Pass	2NT	3NT

FOOTNOTES

1. Stayman and transfers can be used after a 2NT opening, or 2♣-2♦-2NT/3NT.
2. Stayman can be used with 0-7 points when short in clubs, planning to pass opener's rebid.
3. With four hearts and four spades, opener bids 2♥ in response to Stayman, bidding *up the line*.
4. Other meanings can be assigned to jump responses of 3♣ and 3♦ (signoff, or forcing).
5. Some partnerships also use transfer bids at the four level (Texas transfers).

Color Key: ▮ Forcing/Game ▯ Invitational ▮ Signoff ▮ Conventional

	RESPONSE	POINTS	DESCRIPTION
SLAM 33+ PTS.	6NT	13 - 15	Balanced (usually)
	5NT	16	Inviting grand slam
	4NT	11 - 12	Inviting opener to bid slam
GAME 26+ PTS.	4♠	4 - 10	Six-card or longer suit
	4♡	4 - 10	Six-card or longer suit[5]
	4♦		Partnership agreement[5]
	4♣	13+	Gerber: asking for aces
GAME 25+ PTS.	3NT	4 - 10	Balanced (usually)
	3♠		Partnership agreement
	3♥	0+	Transfer to 3♠; five or more spades[1]
	3♦		Transfer to 3♥; five or more hearts[1]
	3♣	4+	Stayman: asking for a major suit[1]
	Pass	0 - 3	Balanced (usually)

RESPONDING TO 2NT

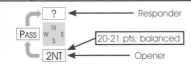
? ← Responder
PASS
20-21 pts; balanced
2NT ← Opener

	RESPONSE	POINTS	DESCRIPTION
SLAM 33+ PTS.	6NT	18 - 19	Balanced (usually)
	5NT	20 - 21	Inviting grand slam
	4NT	16 - 17	Inviting opener to bid slam
GAME 26+ PTS.	4♠	10 - 15	Six-card or longer suit
	4♡	10 - 15	Six-card or longer suit[5]
	4♦		Partnership agreement[5]
	4♣	18+	Gerber: asking for aces
GAME 25+ PTS.	3NT	10 - 15	Balanced (usually)
	3♠	16+	Six-card or longer suit; slam interest
	3♥		
	3♦	8 - 9	Good six-card suit[4]
	3♣		
	2NT		Balanced (usually)
	2♠		Relay to 3♣; six or more clubs or diamonds
	2♥	0+	Transfer to 2♠; five or more spades
	2♦		Transfer to 2♥; five or more hearts
	2♣	8+	Stayman: asking for a major suit
	Pass	0 - 7	Balanced (usually)[2]

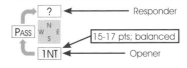
RESPONDING TO 1NT

? ← Responder
PASS
15-17 pts; balanced
1NT ← Opener

Artificial 2♣ Opening and Responses

Opening bids at the one level are not *forcing*. Opening weak two-bids (2♦, 2♥, 2♠) and three level suit bids (3♣, 3♦, 3♥, 3♠) are also not forcing. As a result, all strong hands are opened with an artificial 2♣ bid.

> ### Guideline for Opening 2♣
> - 22+ points or
> - Nine or more tricks

The Artificial 2♦ Response

A response of 2♦ is an *artificial waiting bid*, leaving the maximum room for opener to describe the hand. *Responder's* strength and *distribution* can be shown later in the auction.

Positive Responses

Responder can make an immediate positive response instead of the 2♦ waiting response. This commits the partnership to game.

With about 8 or more points:

- 2♥, 2♠, 3♣, or 3♦ shows a good five-card or longer suit.
- 2NT shows a *balanced* hand (rare).

Opener's Rebid after a 2♦ Response

With a *balanced* hand, opener rebids 2NT with 22-24, 3NT with 25-27, 4NT with 28-30. These are not forcing, and responder uses the same responses as over a notrump opening bid, *Stayman* and *transfers*.

With an *unbalanced* hand, opener bids the longest suit – *higher-ranking* of two five-card or six-card suits. This is a forcing bid.

Responder's Second Bid after Responding 2♦

If opener rebids 2NT or 3NT, showing a balanced hand, responder uses the same methods as after a notrump opening bid.

If opener rebids a suit, responder must bid again[1]. Responder's bid of the *cheaper minor* available at the three level shows a weak hand of about 0-4 points.

Footnotes

1. When opener shows an unbalanced hand, the only time responder can pass below game is if responder shows a weak hand using the *cheaper minor* and opener rebids the same suit.

Color Key: ■ Forcing/Game ■ Invitational ■ Signoff ■ Conventional

	REBID	POINTS	DESCRIPTION
		Other rebids are rare	
GAME	4♥	0 - 4	Four hearts; no A, K, void, or singleton
	4♣/♦		Partnership agreement
	3♠/3NT		
	3♥	5+	Three or more hearts
	3♦		Five or more diamonds
	3♣	0 - 4	Artificial (cheaper minor negative)
	2NT	5+	Balanced
	2♠		Five or more spades

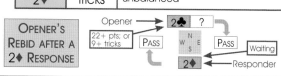

RESPONDER'S SECOND BID

Waiting → 2♦ ? ← Responder

22+ pts or 9+ tricks — PASS · PASS — Unbalanced; five or more hearts

Opener → 2♣ 2♥ ←

	REBID	POINTS	DESCRIPTION
		Other rebids are rare	
	4NT	28 - 30	Balanced
GAME	4♥/♠		Partnership agreement (Rare)
	4♣/♦		
GAME 25+ PTS	3NT	25 - 27	Balanced
	3♥/♠		Partnership agreement (Rare)
	3♦	9+ tricks	Five-card or longer suit, unbalanced
	3♣		
	2NT	22 - 24	Balanced
	2♠	9+ tricks	Five-card or longer suit, unbalanced
	2♥		

ARTIFICIAL 2♣ OPENING AND RESPONSES

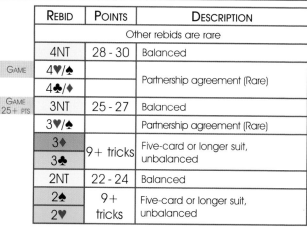

OPENER'S REBID AFTER A 2♦ RESPONSE

Opener → 2♣ ?

22+ pts; or 9+ tricks — PASS · PASS — Waiting

2♦ ← Responder

RESPONSE	POINTS	DESCRIPTION
	Other responses are rare	
3♦	8+	Good five-card or longer suit
3♣		
2NT		Balanced (rare)
2♠		Good five-card or longer suit
2♥		
2♦	0+	Any distribution; waiting

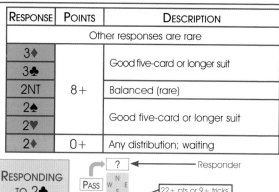

RESPONDING TO 2♣

? ← Responder

PASS

22+ pts or 9+ tricks

2♣ ← Opener

SLAM BIDDING

There is a large bonus for bidding and making a *slam* contract. There are three keys to successful slam bidding:

- Combined strength
- *Fit*
- *Controls*: aces, kings, *voids*, and *singletons*.

COMBINED STRENGTH

To consider bidding a slam, at least one member of the partnership must determine there are about 33 or more combined points:

STRENGTH REQUIREMENT FOR SLAM	
33+ points	Small Slam
37+ points	Grand Slam

For example, if the opening bid is 1NT (15-17) and *responder* has 18 points, responder knows there is at least enough combined strength for a small slam (15 + 18 = 33) but not enough strength for a grand slam (17 + 18 = 35). If responder is unsure, holding 17 points for example, responder can make a slam *invitational* bid, such as *quantitative raise* to 4NT.

FIT

At the slam level, there is little difference between major and minor suits. Both 6♣ and 6♥ receive the same slam bonus. The partnership should consider playing in any eight-card or longer fit. The partnership considers playing in notrump if there is no eight-card or longer fit, or if both hands are *balanced*, or if there is considerable extra strength.

CONTROLS[1]

Even when the partnership has enough strength for slam and has found a suitable fit, there is a third consideration. The partnership doesn't want to be in a grand slam if the opponents can take the first trick with an ace or in a small slam if the opponents can take the first two tricks with two aces, or an ace-king in a suit.

The partnership, therefore, wants to check that it has a sufficient number of aces, and perhaps kings. There are two popular ways to do this. The *Blackwood* convention is used when the partnership has agreed on a trump suit. The *Gerber* convention is typically used when the last bid is a natural 1NT or 2NT.

BLACKWOOD CONVENTION

After a trump suit has been determined, a bid of 4NT asks how many aces partner holds.

RESPONSES TO BLACKWOOD 4NT

5♠	Three aces
5♥	Two aces
5♦	One ace
5♣	Zero or all four aces[2]

If the partnership is missing two aces, it can stop at the five level in the agreed trump suit[3]. If only one ace is missing, a small *slam* can be bid in the agreed trump suit. If the partnership holds all the aces and is interested in a grand slam, a bid of 5NT asks how many kings partner holds.

RESPONSES TO BLACKWOOD 5NT

6NT	Four kings
6♠	Three kings
6♥	Two kings
6♦	One king
6♣	Zero kings

GERBER CONVENTION

After an opening 1NT or 2NT or a natural rebid of 1NT or 2NT, such as 1♦-1♥-2NT, a *jump* to 4♣ asks how many aces partner holds. A subsequent bid of 5♣ asks about kings.

RESPONSES TO GERBER 4♣

4NT	Three aces
4♠	Two aces
4♥	One ace
4♦	Zero or four aces

RESPONSES TO GERBER 5♣

6♣	Four kings
5NT	Three kings
5♠	Two kings
5♥	One king
5♦	Zero kings

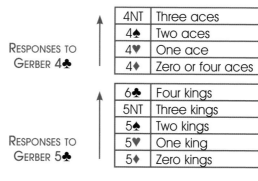

SLAM BIDDING, BLACKWOOD AND GERBER

FOOTNOTES

1. In a trump contract, a *void* can serve the same role as an ace, and a *singleton* can act like a king—stopping the defenders from taking the first two tricks in the suit. Showing voids and singletons involves *control*-showing bids and other conventions beyond the scope of this guide.
2. The 5♣ response to *Blackwood* serves a dual purpose to leave 5NT available to ask for kings.
3. Before using Blackwood, be sure the response won't take the partnership beyond a safe level.

DECLARER PLAY

Before playing to the first trick, declarer should make a plan. There are three suggested stages, the ABC's:

> **A**ssess the Situation
> **B**rowse Declarer's Checklist
> **C**onsider the Order

ASSESS THE SITUATION

- **Goal.** Start by considering the number of tricks required to make the contract, or the number of tricks that can be lost. In 4♥, for example, declarer needs ten tricks or can afford three losers.
- **Sure Tricks/Losers.** Count the sure tricks—winners —those that can be taken without giving up the lead. In a suit contract, consider losers—tricks the opponents can take after gaining the lead.
- **Extra Tricks Needed/Losers to Eliminate.** Compare the number of tricks needed to the sure tricks. In a suit contract, compare the number of losers declarer can afford to the potential losers.

BROWSE DECLARER'S CHECKLIST

When there aren't enough sure tricks, or there are too many losers, declarer looks at the techniques for developing extra tricks and eliminating losers:

DECLARER'S CHECKLIST	
Promotion	
Length	
The Finesse	
Trumping in Dummy	
Discarding Losers	

The first three apply to both notrump and trump contracts. The last two apply only in trump contracts.

PROMOTION: Turning cards into winners by driving out the higher-ranking cards.

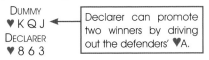

DUMMY
♥ K Q J
DECLARER
♥ 8 6 3

Declarer can promote two winners by driving out the defenders' ♥A.

LENGTH: Continuing to lead a suit until the defenders have no cards left, leaving declarer's remaining cards as winners.

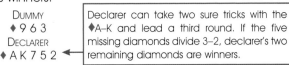

DUMMY
♦ 9 6 3
DECLARER
♦ A K 7 5 2

Declarer can take two sure tricks with the ♦A–K and lead a third round. If the five missing diamonds divide 3–2, declarer's two remaining diamonds are winners.

> GUIDELINE: An odd number of missing cards tends to divide as evenly as possible; an even number of missing cards tends to divide slightly unevenly.

The Finesse: Developing tricks with high cards when the defenders hold higher-ranking cards.

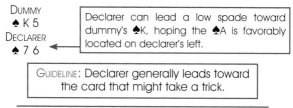

DUMMY
♠ K 5
DECLARER
♠ 7 6

Declarer can lead a low spade toward dummy's ♠K, hoping the ♠A is favorably located on declarer's left.

> GUIDELINE: Declarer generally leads toward the card that might take a trick.

Trumping in Dummy: Gaining a trick by trumping a loser with one of dummy's trumps.

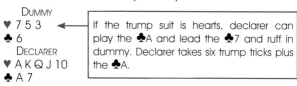

DUMMY
♥ 7 5 3
♣ 6
DECLARER
♥ A K Q J 10
♣ A 7

If the trump suit is hearts, declarer can play the ♣A and lead the ♣7 and ruff in dummy. Declarer takes six trump tricks plus the ♣A.

Discarding Losers: Eliminating losers by discarding them on extra winners in dummy.

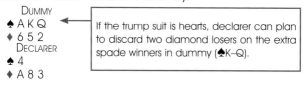

DUMMY
♠ A K Q
♦ 6 5 2
DECLARER
♠ 4
♦ A 8 3

If the trump suit is hearts, declarer can plan to discard two diamond losers on the extra spade winners in dummy (♠K–Q).

CONSIDER THE ORDER

When developing and taking tricks, or eliminating losers, the order the tricks are played can be important. Here are some considerations:

- Take the winners. With enough tricks, take them before something goes wrong.
- Draw trumps. In a suit contract, play the trump suit first unless it is needed for other purposes.
- Keep enough trumps in dummy. When planning to trump losers, it may be necessary to delay drawing trumps.
- Take the losses early. When developing tricks, don't be afraid of losing tricks early, while keeping sure tricks in other suits to regain the lead.
- High card from the short side first. When taking or promoting winners in unevenly-divided suits, it's usually a good idea to start by playing the high cards from the hand with fewer cards.
- Watch the entries. Plan to be in the appropriate hand at the right time.
- Watch the opponents. Be aware of the tricks the defenders may take if they gain the lead.

DECLARER PLAY

DEFENSE

LEADING AGAINST NOTRUMP CONTRACTS

First choose the suit; then choose the appropriate card in the suit.

PARTNER'S SUIT:

- Lead the top of a *doubleton* (♠<u>7</u>–2, ♦J–5).
- Lead the top of touching honors (♥<u>Q</u>–J–5).
- With no *sequence*, lead low[1] (♦K–7–<u>5</u>, ♣8–6–<u>3</u>).

LONGEST SUIT[2,3]:

- With a choice of suits, lead the stronger.
- Lead the top of touching honors from a sequence:
  - A solid sequence (♥<u>K</u>–Q–J–7–4)
  - A broken sequence (♠<u>J</u>–10–8–6)
  - An interior sequence (♦A–<u>J</u>–10–2).
- With no sequence, lead *fourth best* (♣K–J–9–<u>6</u>–4).

LEADING AGAINST SUIT CONTRACTS

First choose the suit – it isn't automatic[4]. Then choose the appropriate card in the suit.

PARTNER'S SUIT:

- Lead the top of a doubleton (♠<u>7</u>–2, ♦J–5).
- Lead the top of touching honors (♥<u>Q</u>–J–5).
- With no sequence, lead low[5] (♣8–6–<u>3</u>, ♥K–9–<u>6</u>).

AN UNBID SUIT:

- Lead the top of a doubleton (♠<u>7</u>–2, ♦J–5).
- Lead the top of touching honors (♥<u>Q</u>–J–5).
- Lead the ace[5] (♠<u>A</u>–J–7–4–2).
- Lead fourth best (♥K–J–7–<u>3</u>, ♠J–9–7–<u>6</u>–3) or low from three cards[6] (♦Q–10–<u>5</u>).

A SINGLETON OR A DOUBLETON - Hoping to get a *ruff*.

A TRUMP - To prevent declarer *ruffing* losers in dummy.

FOOTNOTES

1. If you raised partner's suit, lead top of nothing (♠<u>8</u>–6–5) or low from an honor (♦Q–7–<u>2</u>).
2. Avoid leading the opponents' suits, especially a major suit opened by the opponents.
3. When leading against notrump from a weak hand, an alternative to leading from a long suit is top of nothing (♠<u>9</u>–6–5), hoping to find partner's best suit.
4. Listen for clues from the auction when deciding what to lead.
5. Avoid leading low (away) from an ace against a suit contract.
6. From three low cards, lead the lowest (♥7–4–<u>3</u>). Some partnership prefer to lead the top card (♥<u>7</u>–4–3), or the middle card (♥7–<u>4</u>–3).

SIGNALS

The three types of *signals* in order of priority are:

1) *Attitude Signal*

   When partner leads or when discarding:
   - A high card is encouraging.
   - A low card is discouraging.

2) *Count Signal*

   When declarer plays a suit:
   - A high card followed by a low card shows an even number.
   - A low card followed by a high card shows an odd number.

3) *Suit Preference Signal*

   When attitude and count don't apply:
   - A high card shows preference for the *higher-ranking* of the remaining suits.
   - A low card shows preference for the *lower-ranking* of the remaining suits.

PLANNING THE DEFENSE

Defenders play like declarer:

- If there are enough sure tricks to defeat the contract, take the tricks.
- Otherwise, develop extra tricks using the DEFENDERS' CHECKLIST:

DEFENDERS' CHECKLIST	
Promotion	
Length	
Finesse	
Trumping	

GUIDELINES FOR THE DEFENDERS

- Second hand low ... but take the setting trick.
- Third hand high ... but only as high as necessary.
- Cover an honor with an honor ... if a winner can potentially be promoted in the suit.
- Return partner's suit ... it may not be right but it is never wrong.

GUIDELINE (RULE) OF ELEVEN

When partner leads fourth highest, subtract the pips on the cards from 11. The result is the number of cards in the remaining three hands that are higher than the one led.

Advancer—The partner of a player who makes an overcall or takeout double.

Artificial Waiting Bid—A temporizing bid, such as the 2♦ response to a strong 2♣ opening bid.

Balanced—A hand with no voids, no singletons, and no more than one doubleton.

Bidding Ladder—The order in which bids can be made, starting with 1♣ and ending with 7NT.

Blackwood—An artificial bid of 4NT, after a trump suit has been agreed, to ask for the number of aces partner holds: 5♣=0/4; 5♦=1; 5♥=2; 5♠=3.

Cheaper Minor—An artificial bid of the cheaper minor to show a very weak hand of about 0-3 points after an opening bid of 2♣, a waiting response of 2♦, and opener rebids 2♥, 2♠, or 3♣. Over 3♦, responder bids 3NT.

Control—A holding that prevents the opponents from taking the first two tricks in a suit. An ace or void is a 'first-round' control; a king or a singleton is a 'second-round' control.

Conventional—A bid which conveys a meaning other than what would normally be attributed to it.

Corollary to the Law of Total Tricks—The partnership should generally compete to a level corresponding to the number of combined trumps held by the partnership (e.g. With nine combined trumps, compete to the three level – nine tricks).

Cuebid—An artificial forcing bid in an opponents' suit.

Distribution Points—Valuation points for the trick-taking potential of long suits, or short suits in a trump contract.

Doubleton—A holding of two cards in a suit.

Dummy Points—Points used in place of length points when valuing a hand in support of partner's suit or when making a takeout double.

First Position—The dealer, who is the first player to have the chance to bid or pass.

Fit—A combined holding of eight or more cards in a suit, making it playable as a trump suit.

Forcing—A call that partner is not expected to pass.

Forcing 1NT—Conventional agreement that when opener bids 1♥ or 1♠ in first or second position and the next player passes, a response of 1NT shows about 6-12 points and is forcing for one round. Some partnerships play 1NT, semi-forcing.

Fourth Best—The fourth card from the top in a suit.

Fourth Position—The player to the dealer's right. The fourth player to have a chance to make a call.

Gambling 3NT—An opening bid of 3NT based on the playing tricks from a long solid minor suit rather than high-card points.

Game—A total trick score of 100 or more points.

Game Try—A bid inviting partner to game.

Gerber—A conventional bid of 4♣ asking partner to show the number of aces held. Typically used after a natural notrump opening bid or rebid.

Good Suit—A suit headed by two of the top three honors or three of the top five.

Guideline of 15—In borderline cases in fourth position, the high-card points are added to the number of spades in the hand. If the total is 15 or more, the suggestion is to open; otherwise, to pass.

Guideline of 20—In borderline cases in first or second position, the high-card points are added to the number of cards in the two longest suits. If the total is 20 or more, consider opening the bidding.

High-Card Points (HCPs)—The value of high cards in a hand: Ace, 4; King, 3; Queen, 2; Jack, 1.

Higher-Ranking—A suit that ranks higher on the Bidding Ladder than another suit.

Inverted Minors—An agreement that a single raise of opener's minor to the two level is strong and a jump raise to the three level is weak.

Invitational—A bid which encourages partner to continue bidding while allowing partner to pass.

Jacoby 2NT—An artificial response of 2NT to an opening bid of 1♥ or 1♠ that shows support for opener's suit and enough strength to take the partnership to at least game.

Jump—A bid at more than the minimum level available. Such as a jump raise, jump rebid, jump overcall, or jump shift to a new suit.

Length Points—The valuation assigned to long suits in a hand: five-card suit, 1 point; six-card suit, 2 points; seven-card suit, 3 points; eight-card suit, 4 points.

Limit Raise—A raise of partner's suit from the one level to the three level that invites partner to game.

Lower-Ranking—A suit that ranks lower on the Bidding Ladder than another suit.

Michaels Cuebid—A direct cuebid of an opponent's opening bid to show a distributional takeout.

Negative Double—The conventional use of responder's overcall as a takeout double rather than a penalty double.

Old Suit—A suit previously bid by the partnership.

Overcall—A bid made after the opponents have opened the bidding.

Partscore—A contract that does not receive a game bonus if made.

Pass—A call specifying that a player does not want to bid at that turn. Bidding messages don't usually apply.

Passed Hand—A player who passed when given an opportunity to open the bidding and, therefore, is assumed to hold fewer than 12 points.

Penalty Double—A double made with the expectation of defeating the opponents' contract.

Playing Tricks—Tricks a hand can be expected to take if the partnership buys the contract.

Preemptive Bid—A jump bid made to interfere with the opponents by taking away bidding room.

Quantitative Raise—A raise of partner's suit or notrump bid that asks partner to continue to game or slam with maximum strength.

Redouble—A call that increases the bonuses for making or defeating a contract that has already been doubled.

Re-raise—Opener's rebid of the original suit after it has been raised by responder (e.g. 1♥-2♥-3♥).

Responder—The partner of the opening bidder.

Reverse by Opener—A rebid by opener of a new suit that prevents responder from returning to opener's original suit at the two level (e.g. 1♦-1♠-2♥).

Ruff(ing)—Play a trump to a trick when holding no cards in the suit led.

Second Position—Player to the left of the dealer who is second to have a chance to bid or pass.

Semi-balanced—A hand that might be suitable for a notrump contract even though it has more than one doubleton: 5-4-2-2 or 6-3-2-2 distribution.

Sequence—Three or more consecutive cards in a suit. May be a solid, broken, or interior sequence.

Signals—Conventional plays made by the defenders to give each other information.

Signoff—A call suggesting that partner pass.

Singleton—A holding of one card in a suit.

Slam—A contract to take twelve (small slam) or thirteen (grand slam) tricks.

Splinter Bid—A conventional double jump in a new suit to show support for partner's suit and a singleton or void in the suit bid.

Standard—Bidding system based on five-card major openings and a strong 1NT opening.

Stayman—An artificial response of 2♣ to an opening bid of 1NT, asking if opener has a four-card major suit. Stayman can also be used after a notrump overcall or higher-level notrump bids.

Stopper—A holding that is likely to prevent the opponents from immediately taking all the tricks in the suit.

Takeout Double—A double that asks partner to bid an unbid suit.

Texas Transfers—A similar convention to Jacoby transfers. After a 1NT or 2NT opening, a jump to 4♦ asks opener to bid 4♥; a jump to 4♥ asks opener to bid 4♠.

Third Position—Dealer's partner.

Transfer Bid—A bid that shows length in a different suit. For example, a response of 2♦ to an opening 1NT bid asks opener to bid 2♥.

Two-Over-One Game Force (2/1)—A partnership agreement that, without interference, a non-jump two-over-one response in a new suit is forcing to game if responder has not passed initially.

Unbalanced Hand—A hand with a void, a singleton, or more than one doubleton.

Unusual Notrump—A conventional notrump bid to show a two-suited hand.

Up the Line—Bidding the cheapest of two or more four-card suits.

Void—A holding of zero cards in a suit.

Vulnerability—In duplicate or Chicago scoring, vulnerability is assigned to each deal. Bonuses and penalties are greater when a partnership is vulnerable than when it is non-vulnerable.

SCORES

Contract	Made	Not Vulnerable			Vulnerable		
		Undoubled	Doubled	Redoubled	Undoubled	Doubled	Redoubled
3♥/3♠	7	260	930	1560	260	1530	2560
	6	230	830	1360	230	1330	2160
	5	200	730	1160	200	1130	1760
	4	170	630	960	170	930	1360
	3	140	530	760	140	730	960
3♣/3♦	7	190	870	1440	190	1470	2440
	6	170	770	1240	170	1270	2040
	5	150	670	1040	150	1070	1640
	4	130	570	840	130	870	1240
	3	110	470	640	110	670	840
2NT	7	270	990	1680	270	1690	2880
	6	240	890	1480	240	1490	2480
	5	210	790	1280	210	1290	2080
	4	180	690	1080	180	1090	1680
	3	150	590	880	150	890	1280
	2	120	490	680	120	690	880
2♥/2♠	7	260	970	1640	260	1670	2840
	6	230	870	1440	230	1470	2440
	5	200	770	1240	200	1270	2040
	4	170	670	1040	170	1070	1640
	3	140	570	840	140	870	1240
	2	110	470	640	110	670	840
2♣/2♦	7	190	680	1560	190	1180	2760
	6	170	580	1360	170	980	2360
	5	150	480	1160	150	780	1960
	4	130	380	960	130	580	1560
	3	110	280	760	110	380	1160
	2	90	180	560	90	180	760
1NT	7	270	780	1760	270	1380	3160
	6	240	680	1560	240	1180	2760
	5	210	580	1360	210	980	2360
	4	180	480	1160	180	780	1960
	3	150	380	960	150	580	1560
	2	120	280	760	120	380	1160
	1	90	180	560	90	180	760
1♥/1♠	7	260	760	1720	260	1360	3120
	6	230	660	1520	230	1160	2720
	5	200	560	1320	200	960	2320
	4	170	460	1120	170	760	1920
	3	140	360	920	140	560	1520
	2	110	260	720	110	360	1120
	1	80	160	520	80	160	720
1♣/1♦	7	190	740	1430	190	1340	2630
	6	170	640	1230	170	1140	2230
	5	150	540	1030	150	940	1830
	4	130	440	830	130	740	1430
	3	110	340	630	110	540	1030
	2	90	240	430	90	340	630
	1	70	140	230	70	140	230

Contract	Made	Not Vulnerable			Vulnerable		
		Undoubled	Doubled	Redoubled	Undoubled	Doubled	Redoubled
7NT	7	1520	1790	2280	2220	2490	2980
7♥/7♠	7	1510	1770	2240	2210	2470	2940
7♣/7♦	7	1440	1630	1960	2140	2330	2660
6NT	7	1020	1330	1860	1470	1880	2510
	6	990	1230	1660	1440	1680	2110
6♥/6♠	7	1010	1310	1820	1460	1860	2470
	6	980	1210	1620	1430	1660	2070
6♣/6♦	7	940	1190	1580	1390	1740	2230
	6	920	1090	1380	1370	1540	1830
5NT	7	520	870	1440	720	1270	2040
	6	490	770	1240	690	1070	1640
	5	460	670	1040	660	870	1240
5♥/5♠	7	510	850	1400	710	1250	2000
	6	480	750	1200	680	1050	1600
	5	450	650	1000	650	850	1200
5♣/5♦	7	440	750	1200	640	1150	1800
	6	420	650	1000	620	950	1400
	5	400	550	800	600	750	1000
4NT	7	520	910	1520	720	1410	2320
	6	490	810	1320	690	1210	1920
	5	460	710	1120	660	1010	1520
	4	430	610	920	630	810	1120
4♥/4♠	7	510	890	1480	710	1390	2280
	6	480	790	1280	680	1190	1880
	5	450	690	1080	650	990	1480
	4	420	590	880	620	790	1080
4♣/4♦	7	190	810	1320	190	1310	2120
	6	170	710	1120	170	1110	1720
	5	150	610	920	150	910	1320
	4	130	510	720	130	710	920
3NT	7	520	950	1600	720	1550	2600
	6	490	850	1400	690	1350	2200
	5	460	750	1200	660	1150	1800
	4	430	650	1000	630	950	1400
	3	400	550	800	600	750	1000

PENALTY POINTS

Down	Not Vulnerable			Vulnerable		
	Undoubled	Doubled	Redoubled	Undoubled	Doubled	Redoubled
13	650	3500	7000	1300	3800	7600
12	600	3200	6400	1200	3500	7000
11	550	2900	5800	1100	3200	6400
10	500	2600	5200	1000	2900	5800
9	450	2300	4600	900	2600	5200
8	400	2000	4000	800	2300	4600
7	350	1700	3400	700	2000	4000
6	300	1400	2800	600	1700	3400
5	250	1100	2200	500	1400	2800
4	200	800	1600	400	1100	2200
3	150	500	1000	300	800	1600
2	100	300	600	200	500	1000
1	50	100	200	100	200	400

BRIDGE AT A GLANCE

BRIDGE AT A GLANCE is a quick reference of the material in the award-winning Audrey Grant Bridge Basics series. These summaries work in conjunction with the books which present the reasoning behind the guidelines.

Audrey Grant has an international reputation in the field of bridge education. Her vision and commitment have been key to the success of the Audrey Grant Better Bridge series of books, the Better Bridge magazine, festivals, the Online Interactive Daily Bridge Column, lessons, and practice deals. She works with the game's best theorists to make sure the material is current and of the highest quality. Grant has received many awards for the quality of her material and was recently inducted into the Bridge Hall of Fame.

David Lindop is an integral part of the Audrey Grant Better Bridge products and is essential to their success. He is a popular writer and an expert who competes regularly in world championships. David is an active member of the bridge community, holding the record for chairing the second-largest bridge tournament in the world, attracting more than 22,000 tables in play.

For a complete list of Audrey Grant products, cruises, and festivals visit: www.AudreyGrant.com

Audrey's books, cards and the Better Bridge Magazine are available from:

Baron Barclay Bridge Supplies
3600 Chamberlain Lane, Suite 206
Louisville, KY 40241 • Tel: 800-274-2221 • 502-426-0410
sales@baronbarclay.com • www.baronbarclay.com

ISBN 978-1-944201-40-1
51195

$11.95 US

9 781944 201401